How a Young Brave Survived

as told by **Adeline Mathias**

edited by **Penny Hamilton**

illustrated by **Francis Auld**
and **Debbie Joseph**

developed by
Kootenai Culture Committee
Confederated Salish and Kootenai Tribes

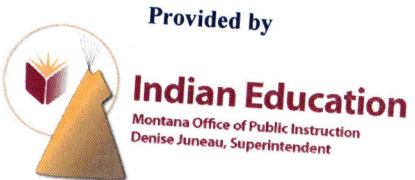

Provided by

Indian Education
Montana Office of Public Instruction
Denise Juneau, Superintendent

published by
Salish Kootenai College Press
Pablo, Montana
distributed by University of Nebraska Press
Lincoln, Nebraska

Kootenai Culture Committee Staff during 1986 :
Patricia Hewankorn, Director
Betty Nichols
Sophie Matt
Sarah Bufton
Nancy Joseph
Clarinda Burke

Cover design by Wyatt Design, Helena, MT.
Cover drawing by Debbie Joseph.

Library of Congress Cataloging-in-Publication Data:
Mathias, Adeline, 1910-2007.
    How a young brave survived / as told by Adeline Mathias ; edited by Penny Hamilton ; illustrated by Francis Auld and Debbie Joseph.
    p. cm.
    Originally published: 1986.
    ISBN 978-1-934594-04-9
    1. Kootenai Indians--Montana--History--Juvenile literature. 2. Wilderness survival--Montana--History--Juvenile literature. 3. Survival skills--Montana--History--Juvenile literature. I. Hamilton, Penny (Penny S.) II. Auld, Francis, ill. III. Finley, Debbie Joseph, 1953- ill. IV. Title.
    E99.K85M38 2009
    978.6--dc22   2009037637

This printing reset and reprinted 2009 by Salish Kootenai College Press, PO Box 70, Pablo, MT 59855

Distributed by University of Nebraska Press, 1111 Lincoln Mall, Lincoln, NE 68588-0630, order 1-800-755-1105, www.nebraskapress.unl.edu.

*T*his is a true Kootenai story that happened many years ago. It isn't a legend.

Many years ago, during the Indian conflicts, when a warrior was preparing for battle against his enemy he would perform a ceremonial dance before departing. He would take a rawhide from his lodge outside and commence to beat on it. When the other warriors in the camp heard the drumbeat they would join the drummers. They knew the meaning of this ceremony.

Throughout Indian war times a Kootenai warrior would never leave for battle without first performing the Rawhide Beat Dance. The warriors drummed from evening until dawn. They had to be finished by daybreak so they could depart for war. It is traditional that the Kootenai didn't have war at night.

Today, at the annual Pow-wows, the Rawhide Beat Dance is still held. The name has been changed to the "Canvas Dance." The old timers have great honor and respect for this ceremony, it has an important meaning. The young adults of today, however, don't really know what it signifies and no longer honor or respect this dance.

Women, whether they had families or not, accompanied the war party even though they knew the danger they were facing. The women and children were often killed also on these ventures. The women accompanied the warriors to mend worn-out moccasins. Some of the young adults volunteered to go along to pack water and help with other chores.

The Kootenai Indians traveled as far northwest as the Libby area, Jennings and on into Canada. At that time there was no boundary, the land was considered part of their territory. They camped beside the various lakes in these places, such as McGregor Lake, Thompson Lake, Crystal Lake, Horseshoe Lake and Bitterroot Lake. The Kootenai people had Indian names for all these lakes as they considered them part of their territory and their hunting grounds.

Long ago the Kootenais didn't have horses, they traveled on foot. The horses weren't available until a much later date. Availability of the horses created more conflict between tribes as horse stealing came about.

When a warrior intended to steal horses from the enemy camp circle he always looked for the best horses to steal. He cut the ropes and drove the horses out. If he wasn't caught he would drive them back to his country. He thought he was great and was proud of himself. However, if he was caught it instigated war.

Whenever a warrior killed an enemy, it isn't that he is honored. The one who scalps the dead is the one who is considered brave and courageous. The warrior would take the scalp back to the camp and display it on a staff while all the warriors gathered to do the "Scalp Dance."

While in the enemy country the Kootenai slept lightly and listened intently, fearing a sneak attack.

It has been said that there will never be war on this continent we now live on, that we will never hear gunshots or mortar shell blasts. We have been told that we will always live in peace on this continent.

One day, late in the fall, a group of Kootenai warriors decided to go to the Blackfeet country and make war. When evening came they did the Rawhide Beat Dance, then in the early dawn they left camp and started their long journey.

One warrior took his thirteen-year-old son along, thinking it was time for him to experience warfare. He wanted to teach him to be a courageous and brave warrior. The group traveled continuously and spent many days and nights in the mountains before reaching Blackfeet country. They traveled far out into the plains. Late one evening they stopped for the night.

In the early morning they were unexpectedly attacked by the enemy. They were greatly outnumbered and all were killed, except for the young boy who managed to escape. He escaped by walking and hiding in the gullies. He didn't have a weapon, no bow and arrows. The only thing he had was a small buckskin pouch fastened to his belt, much like the one adults used. They all carried buckskin pouches for flint and other small items they may need. The young brave had only an animal skin wrapped around him.

He furtively walked until he reached the mountains. It was late in the fall and snow had already fallen in the higher mountainous areas.

He continued walking, never stopping to get any sleep. His idea was to get as far away from the battle area and the enemy as he could. He was fearful the enemy may have followed him. The enemy knew he had escaped. He did not take the trail they traveled before but took a different route. The Kootenai had many different trails they used when going to the enemy country.

As he struggled along after two days of walking, he became exhausted, cold and hungry. He only had a small fur wrap and his moccasins were wet from walking in the snow. He couldn't remember when he had last eaten, it had to be before the battle. He thought to himself as he walked, "I am so afraid I am going to die, either from starvation or freezing to death." After walking a short distance, he sat and rested. It was getting late, he had to find a place to rest for the night. He found a large tree with boughs that touched the ground. He broke off the branches, spread them under the tree and lay down, covering himself with the animal skin he had.

The next morning he awakened and continued on his journey. He walked for a short distance and had to sit and rest, he was so tired and hungry. After he rested, he continued on. He felt so sad because he was so far from home.

He became exhausted, sat down to rest again, and dozed off. A strange sound awoke him. He heard singing. He sat awhile before opening his eyes. He was thinking of how pitiful he was, far away from home, in a strange country; how cold and hungry he was. When he opened his eyes he saw a little snowbird perched on a branch chirping. The boy dug around under the snow for rocks. He found some but they were frozen solid in the ground. He dug a rock out and with all his strength threw it at the bird. To his surprise he knocked it down.

As the bird struggled on the ground the boy felt sorry for it. After the bird quit moving he picked it up and thought to himself, "If I pluck the feathers and eat it, it won't fill me. It's too small, and I'm so hungry." With bird in hand he sat thinking, "I know how to set a snare. I wonder if I'll be able to trap a small animal such as a weasel or a rabbit?" He pulled off his moccasin strings, stretched them as much as he could, then went looking for a good spot to build a support for the bird bait. After he finished the support he put the bird inside and set the snare. Any small animal catching the scent of the bird would go through the snare and into the support. When it takes the bait out, the snare will tighten around the animal's neck, choking it.

After he finished setting the trap he thought, "I may as well get ready for the night. I'll build a shelter." He gathered some wood, shrubs, and small trees that he could break easily. He set them up for support and made the shelter sturdy. He built it in a half circle and rounded the top, similar to a sweat house. He broke tree boughs, spread them around the inside for a bed. It was late when he finished. He went to bed tired, cold, and hungry. When he lay down he thought, "If it doesn't blizzard tonight, I'll be lucky."

When he awoke it was daybreak. The first thing that came to mind was the predicament he was in. He was feeling sad. He still had his pouch and the things he needed to start a fire but he wanted to wait and use them when he really needed to. He got up, put his animal skin wrap on and left to check his trap. As he approached the trap, he noticed the support was down. He had trapped a weasel! This made him happy, now he would have something to eat. He re-set his trap using the same bait. Taking his kill, he went back to his shelter.

The young brave walked around the area and went down the
hill. He came to a creek which was snow-covered. It took him
awhile to clear off the snow in order to get a drink of water. This
was his first drink since his escape from the war party. After he had
his fill of water he walked until he came to a cluster of cottonwood
trees. He looked around and found some tinder. The tinder was
quite thin but he tore some pieces out and walked back to the
creek. He gathered a few small rocks and a larger flat rock which
he took back to his shelter. He gathered some dry wood and pitch
as well.

He quickly made a fireplace and broke the pitch and wood into small pieces. He placed the cottonwood tinder on the flat rock, took out his flint, and rubbed the flint and rock together over the cottonwood tinder until it caught on fire. He put the tinder under the dry wood and pitch and blew on it until it started to burn good. Soon he had a big warm fire.

He carefully skinned the weasel, he wanted to save the skin and sinew. When he finished skinning the weasel he turned the skin inside out and put it over a piece of thin wood to dry. He saved the intestines for bait.

He roasted the small animal and had his first meal since his escape. He felt so much better after his meal. He spent the rest of the day gathering more wood and pitch. By evening he had a good supply of firewood. Before he retired for the night he put large pieces of wood in the fire so there would be hot ashes and sparks in the morning.

When he awoke in the morning he went to check his trap. This time he caught a rabbit. He re-set the support and snare. He took the rabbit back to his shelter and skinned it. He used the same routine with the rabbit as he did the weasel. He couldn't eat the entire rabbit. He had to save the rest for another meal.

He sat for awhile and thought, "Since I have something to eat for another day, I wonder if I should start home. I have traveled quite a distance. Will I be able to cross the mountains without getting lost? Will I freeze to death or die of starvation trying to find my way home?" He finally decided to spend another night and he would make up his mind in the morning as to what he would do.

The next morning he was up at daybreak. He ate what was left of the cooked rabbit from the day before. After he finished his meal he went to check his trap. This time he caught a larger rabbit. He carefully dressed it out, saving the sinew and intestines. The sinew was longer and stronger than the first.

He began looking for a young cedar tree from which to make a bow and arrows. He was going to use the sinew for a bow string but would have to splice it together to make it long enough for his bow. He thought he would hunt big animals when he finished his weapon. He re-set his trap again, he had decided to stay awhile longer.

Early the next morning he went hunting. He hadn't gone far when he saw a fawn. He aimed and shot. The fawn staggered until it fell. He was happy that he would have something different to eat other than rabbit.

He packed his kill back to his camp. Although he was only a thirteen-year-old lad, he was capable of doing adult work. Indian boys, years ago, were all smart, they were hunting at the age of eight. He had a thin piece of flat rock which he had sharpened to cut up the meat with. He skinned the fawn and cut up the meat. He saved the brains to use for tanning later. He did not want to waste any of the animal, he was being conservative, he had experienced hunger too long. He placed the meat in the snow where it would keep for a long time without spoiling.

He cooked some of the meat. While he was eating he thought to himself, "Since I have enough fresh meat I could cut some up and smoke it. It would be easier to pack with me. I could take my time traveling, stopping along the way, make my shelter and stay for a day or two before continuing my long journey. I'm far away from the enemy, I feel safe now."

Finally he decided to stay. He gathered all the material he needed to build another shelter. He needed a bigger and sturdier one to hold up under heavy snowfall. He got all the supports for the shelter set up, then he gathered some boughs to spread over the top and on the sides. He left an opening at the top for a smoke escape.

Meanwhile, his people at home were getting worried about the warriors since they had not returned. Another group left the camp to go search for them, not realizing that they had all been killed and only the young brave survived. After many days of traveling they reached the Blackfeet country. They traveled far out into the plains and finally reached the site of the massacre. They returned home feeling sadness in their hearts for their fallen warriors.

In the meantime, the young brave completed his shelter, he had gathered more boughs and spread them inside his shelter for flooring and his bed. It was warm and comfortable. He spent many days gathering wood and pitch, he wanted enough to last for awhile.

He commenced tanning the fawn skin. He often watched his mother tan and had knowledge of how it was done. He made a flesh scraper out of a deer rib which he used to scrape the remaining meat from the skin. He then spread the skin on the snow to keep it moist. The next day he scraped the skin with a piece of thin rock and left it to dry. He soaked the skin and followed the same procedure as before until it was ready for brain tanning. He rubbed the cooked brains over the skin, rolled it up and set it near the fire where it would stay warm. The brains would penetrate the skin and soften it. In a day or two he scraped the hide again, following the same method as before, and in a matter of a short time he finished tanning the fawn skin. The tanning process took many days to complete, but it made a very comfortable and warm robe, it was worth all the effort.

During the time the fawn skin was drying the young warrior would go hunting and each time he would bring home more meat to be dried and stored away. The hides he would tan for use for rugs and robes. He also wanted to make a pair of snowshoes he needed for his trip home.

One day he went hunting and killed two large bucks. He was happy, he could tan the hides to use for his garments and moccasins. He had saved all the sinew from his previous kill to use to sew his garments with. All he would need now was an awl which he would make later.

He dragged one buck back to his shelter and after resting, he decided to go after the other buck. He didn't want to leave it in the mountains too long, he was afraid the coyotes would get to it and eat it up. He was going to dry all the meat again, he didn't want to go hungry. He dressed out the bucks and as before saved everything edible. The sinew he would stretch and dry to use for stitching his garments. He made an awl from a small bone of a deer and worked it down with a rock until it had a fine point. He used this to punch holes to stitch his leggings, shirt and moccasins with the sinew.

He tanned the two hides that he wanted his garments made from. He had an idea how to tan the skins, he watched his mother numerous times when she tanned. He used a deer rib to scrape the skins with. In a short time, he finished tanning the two skins. He set these aside, they were for the garments that he needed.

He continued hunting and bringing his kill home. He was stocked with meat, he wouldn't go hungry during the winter months. It had snowed considerably all this time and was getting colder.

He made a bigger, much stronger bow and arrows and a pair of snowshoes. When he finished he took the items and left his camp. He thought, "If I can't find what I'm looking for, I'll have to sleep under a tree."

He traveled on and on. It was getting late so he looked for a place to spend the night. He found a large tree with branches that hung low to the ground. He broke off some boughs and used them to make a bed for himself under a tree.

The next morning, after he finished his meat, he continued his journey. He was looking for a rugged, mountainous area where there would be a bear den. If he could get a bear he would tan the skin and the meat he could use to supplement his food supply.

He commenced looking for bear markings. When he saw markings of what he thought to be a bear cave he began poking in it. If there was a bear in the den and the growl sounded hollow, he knew it would be a grizzly den. If it sounded solid it would be a black bear's den. He crawled in and killed the bear then pulled it out of the cave. He gutted it out and dragged it home. The bear wasn't too difficult to drag because of the snow-covered ground. It took him two days to drag the bear back to his campsite.

It was late in the day when he reached his campsite so he waited until the next day to skin the bear. He cut up some of the meat to smoke but the rest he buried in the snow to keep for future use. He was planning to cook some on hot charcoal. (Meat has a different flavor when cooked various ways.) The fat, he cut into strips and hung on the rack over the fire. He was planning to tan the hide later.

After smoking the meat he began to tan the hide. He tanned the bear skin the same way he had tanned the fawn skin, leaving the hair on. He had decided not to hunt anymore, so he had plenty of time to tan the bear skin. He was anxious to finish it, he wanted to use it to keep him warm at night.

He had everything he needed to survive the cold days ahead. His meat supply was plentiful. He had robes that he made from the fawn skin and the bear hide. His shelter was larger and warmer, he was very comfortable and content.

He wanted to fish but felt he was too busy with his other work and couldn't find the time. He was hungry for something different to eat than meat. After he finished tanning the bear skin he had time to do some fishing.

He made a fish line out of sinew. He rolled the sinew with the palms of his hands to make it long but still had to splice it to get the length needed. He took a piece of deer bone and worked it down with a sharp rock, shaping it like a hook. After he finished the hook he went down the hillside to the creek where he got his drinking water from, to fish.

He caught some nice trout which he took back and roasted. He enjoyed his meal. Whenever he got hungry for fish he went fishing.

Many days went by, finally it was spring but the snow had not melted. His food supply had lasted through the winter months. He often thought of his mother and relatives, wishing he was home with them.

In the meantime at the camp, the boy's mother was still mourning for her son and husband. She was feeling sad. She was thinking that she would never see them again.

When his meat supply was running low he decided to go home. He made pemmican from the meat he had left and put it into a buckskin bag that he had made. Early the next morning he rolled up his fur robes and, packing them on his back, left his winter home to find his way back to his family's camp. He traveled for days and days, sleeping under big trees when it became too dark to travel. When he made it across the mountains there wasn't much snow on the ground, so he removed his snowshoes, he didn't need them any longer.

As he traveled he wondered if he was heading in the right direction or if he would ever find the camp where his mother and relatives lived. The Kootenais didn't have one encampment for all but scattered throughout an area.

He wondered if the camp he left was still in the same place or if his family had moved to another site. He decided to go to the campsite which he had left. Many days and nights later he reached the camp. He stood and looked over the campsite, dropped his pack and walked to the nearest camp. When he entered the lodge he took everyone by surprise. The people in the camp were shocked to see him.

The men of the camp remarked to the young brave, "We all thought that there weren't any survivors after the battle." The young boy replied, "It is true, all the warriors were killed. I managed to escape. I barely survived the winter. I have been living in the mountains." The young brave then asked if his mother was still living and where could he find her. The man pointed toward her camp. The man told him not to go to his mother's lodge yet, that someone would go and tell her the news. He told the boy, "Your mother is sad, she mourns for you and your father. It is best that I tell her before you go there."

The man left. When he reached the mother's lodge, he entered. He sat down, he didn't know how to approach her with the news without exciting her too much. Finally, after pondering for a moment, he told the mother, "I've brought you good news. It is something impossible but true. Your son has returned, he is alive and well." The mother asked him to repeat what he had said. The man repeated, "I said your son has returned, alive and unharmed. He came to my lodge and inquired about you. Come with me."

The young brave's mother got up, grabbed her fur wrap, and walked with the man to his lodge. When she entered she saw her son sitting at the rear of the lodge. She ran to him and they embraced each other. She was very happy to see him, as well as everyone else in the camp.

The young brave told the people that he had left his pack a short distance away and that he was going after it. He soon returned with his bundle and untied it and handed his mother the bear robe. He told her, "I made this for you." He untied the skin bag and showed her the meat inside.

The men went around the encampment announcing that the young brave had returned. The people shouted with joy. His friends and relatives were all happy to see him and they joined him for a celebration. The young brave shared his pemmican with them.

One night there was a social gathering at a lodge in the encampment. The young brave joined the group and related to them his experiences while he was gone and how he survived the long winter months.

As the boy grew older his tribesmen highly respected him. He grew up to be a great and powerful man.

The story you have read has been related from time to time and generation to generation. It wasn't sheer luck that the brave survived this ordeal. The snowbird had given him strength, power, and courage to survive. This happened to let the people know that there is spiritual power and it will help when it is needed.

Glossary

awl – a tool with a sharpened end used to make holes in buckskin or rawhide.

ceremonial – an action or event that follows traditional customs.

commenced – started; began.

conservative – careful; moderate.

flint – hard quartz that is used to create a spark to start a fire.

furtively – secretly; with stealth

gullies – ditches or trenches that have been made by water.

instigated – caused.

leggings – coverings for the legs made from buckskin.

massacre – the murder or killing of a group of people under particularly cruel circumstances.

mourning – the period of sadness and sorrow after someone's death.

pitch – sticky residue from conifer trees that catches fire easily.

pondering – carefully thinking.

predicament – a difficult or problematic situation.

signifies – indicates meaning and importance.

sinew – thread made from the tendons of an animal.

snare – a hunting trap that uses a noose to catch small animals.

supplement – add to.

tinder – material suitable for starting a fire.

ventures – risky or dangerous activities.

Afterword

This story was told by a Kootenai elder, Adeline Mathias, when she was 75 years of age. Adeline died in 2007 at the age of 96. This story was related to her by her great grandparents, many years ago. Therefore, this event may have occurred in the middle 1700's.

It is a true story that actually happened when the Kootenai were camped in Jennings, Montana. It was from these camping grounds that the Kootenai warriors left to go across the mountains to have warfare with their enemy, the Blackfeet. This was the camp the young brave returned to after wintering in the mountains. He was the lone survivor after the massacre that killed his father and the other warriors.

The Kootenai, years ago, roamed the northwest Montana territory and have been known to travel into Canada. At that time there wasn't a boundary, these areas were known as Kootenai territory.

The Blackfeet, their enemy, had kidnapped a young Kootenai maiden, who later married a Plains Indian brave. The woman, not wanting to forget her language, spoke to her children in her native tongue. Her children, as they grew older also married into the Plains tribes. That was why Kootenai-speaking Indians were found throughout the plains across the mountains.

Adeline Mathias
1910-2007